LET'S CELEBRAT

MOTHER
AND
SON

TOGETHER

A SHARED JOURNAL FOR
TEEN BOYS & THEIR MOMS

sourcebooks
eXplore

To Niklas and Linden

To Louie and Max, whose moms brought magic to this book with me.

Art by Niklas (age 8) and Linden (age 5)

Published by Sourcebooks eXplore, an imprint of Sourcebooks Kids
P.O. Box 4410, Naperville, Illinois 60567-4410
(630) 961-3900
sourcebookskids.com

Source of Production: PrintPlus Limited, Shenzhen, Guangdong Province, China
Date of Production: March 2023
Run Number: 5030196

Printed and bound in China.
PP 10 9 8 7 6 5 4 3 2 1

CLEARING THE PATH

It was late July, and my brother Todd swung a snow shovel over his shoulder and strolled out of his bedroom.

We were supposed to be cleaning our rooms while Mom was at the grocery store. The ultimatum was clean up or lose screen time. *All of it.* But Todd hadn't been frantically cleaning. He'd been playing computer games!

When Mom walked in with arms of groceries, Todd ran to her side, offloading the bags. "Let me help," he said. "Then you can see my spic-and-span room!"

Mom's eyes sparkled as he opened his bedroom door and waved her in.

"Ta-da!" he said, grinning.

My brother's room was spotless. Dirty clothes—gone. Cups, plates, and snack wrappers—vanished. Books, papers, and pens—nope! My brother had really done it.

Then Todd gulped as a baseball rolled out from under his bed. We all looked at the ball's path, and that's when we could see: Everything that used to be spread across his floor had been rapidly shoved beneath his bed in a giant, compressed heap.

"You *snow shoveled* your room?" I whispered.

Todd ignored me, still hoping Mom hadn't noticed.

But moms always do. She walked over to the bed and got down on her hands and knees. She slowly lifted his blanket.

Then Mom began to laugh. Tears filled her eyes as she tried to speak. "Todd, you definitely didn't *clean* your room. But you sure *cleared* it!"

Sometimes, a teen boy needs a mom who takes his ideas in stride.

A teenage boy is a lot like a snowplow driver navigating his first blizzard. The road looks the same as before, yet it's also completely different. His rig is bigger and bulkier. He's trying to follow the right path, but nothing is clear anymore. He's outgrown the safe perimeters of childhood. He's exploring when it's okay to push back, challenge authority, or express his unique and creative ideas.

Today I'm a mom of two boys. I marvel daily at their ingenuity, and I think back to how difficult it must have been for my mom to let my brother navigate his own course. When my boys make a wrong turn, my primal reaction is to pull out the map and steer them straight. I get so wrapped up in my need to guide that I forget: Sometimes a boy just needs to find his way without his mom.

Keeping a journal together will help both of you become more aware of yourselves and each other. Writing prompts strengthen your sense of compassion as you view the world through each other's unique lenses of age and experience. It's like pulling everything out from under the bed. You've got incredible discoveries, a bit of dust, and a mountain of memories. You get to figure out what matters most.

The other day, Todd and I were visiting our mom. The three of us stood at the living room window, watching the next generation linger outside.

"Hey, Todd," I said, trying to piece together memories. "Remember that day you used the snow shovel to clean your room? Did you ever end up losing screen privileges?"

He thought for a moment. Then his whole body filled with joy as he recalled the memory of that day. "You know, I don't remember," he said. "But I can tell you that I always check under my kids' beds!"

"And you're probably a lot clearer about what 'clean your room' means," Mom added with a chuckle.

He reached over and wrapped his arm around her as she leaned her head on his shoulder.

Family memories like his teenage ingenuity and her love-filled responses are moments that remain in our hearts forever.

These five guideposts will help you get the most from your storycatching time together.

1. SET YOUR OWN RULES.

Throw away every preconceived notion you've heard about journaling, and dive into this book however it works for you and your mom. Flip to any page that strikes the two of you or complete the pages sequentially. Answer questions together over bowls of ice cream or pass the book back and forth in turn. Write a little or a lot. Add or alter anything. If a prompt doesn't resonate with you, cross it out. Cover it up. Write your own.

Your mom's stories go on pages that begin "Dear Mom" or "Mom Writes." Corresponding "Dear Son" and "Son Writes" pages are your opportunity to respond or launch different dialogue. When you see a "Dear Son" page, imagine your mom prompting you: "Hey *your-name-here*, I was wondering..." She's asking the question and awaiting your response below. Then intermixed throughout the book are spaces to doodle, write, and add keepsakes together. Photographs are completely optional.

2. TELL YOUR TRUE STORIES.

When we talk, it's easy to fret about what we perceive others might think or say. Use this journal to focus on your own perspective. Describe how you feel. Portray what you see. Write what you know and admit what you don't. The stories you share don't need to be perfect, and neither do you. Fill the pages with as many silly expressions or inside jokes as you want.

The journals my sons and I share are covered with confusing arrows that navigate across the page because we keep squeezing in more word-heavy ideas or we get carried away drawing. Then the next entry we write might contain just a couple thoughts or quick doodles. We misspell words, cross out sentences, and commit grammatical crimes I know we all learned in elementary school. But you know what? We keep going. I have learned that the best discoveries never come from perfection. They emerge when we let our pens wander across the page.

3. FULLY LISTEN.

Try to understand what each other is really communicating. While you may feel tempted to get angry, point out faults, or lecture in these pages, remember that this journal is your opportunity to peek inside each other's heads and hearts. It's a place to see the world through each other's eyes. Does one of you feel misunderstood? Do you need help or crave connection? Or do you just need to be heard?

Some entries in this journal address things you already know about each other. Many are just for fun. And then there are pages that spur memories from childhood. You may even discover emotions, perspectives, or entire stories you weren't aware of—from each other or yourselves. Respond immediately or give yourselves time to reflect.

4. PLAY ON THESE PAGES!

This journal is your time capsule together, so make it fun. Mark it up with speech bubbles and hand-drawn comic strips. Illustrate with colorful emojis, arrows, and mustaches. Emphasize ideas by underlining words or making bubble letters. Try every pen you find. Write backwards. Decorate with gathered mementos and stickers. Snap photos together and adhere them with glue or double-sided tape. Above all, enjoy the process.

5. GO BEYOND THIS BOOK.

Come to my website for more mother-son storycatching activities and projects. My family loves these corny-sweet videos, punny challenges, and adult coloring pages. These and more are all free at:

katieclemons.com/a/BKpT/

Thanks for letting this journal and me join your journey. Write to me any time howdy@katieclemons.com (I answer all my mail) or tag me on social media **@katierclemons #katieclemonsjournals #motherandsontogether**.

Grab that snow shovel. Clear some space in your day, and... Let's celebrate your story!

LET'S BEGIN HERE

Our full names are

We usually call each other

_____

_____

We are _____ and _____ years old, which are fabulous ages because

_____

_____

We always say these expressions

HERE'S A DRAWING OR PHOTOGRAPH OF YOU AND ME DOING
SOMETHING WE LOVE

Today, we start our story!

Date _____

OUR JOURNAL GUIDELINES

which ☐ **ARE** ☐ **ARE NOT** to be strictly followed

1. Our top focus(es) in this journal will be to

☐ Express our honest thoughts

☐ Use flawless grammar

☐ Abandon perfection and enjoy the process together

☐ Write what we perceive each other wants to read

☐ Create a snapshot of our life right now

☐ _____

Thoughts

_____

_____

_____

2. Why are we interested in journaling together?

_____

_____

_____

3. How often would we like to write back and forth?

_____

_____

_____

4. What could we do if we need more space to write?

_____

_____

_____

5. Do we need to answer the prompts in numerical order?

☐ Yes ☐ No

6. How do we pass our journal back and forth? And how do we let each other know which page to turn to?

_____

_____

_____

7. Can anyone else look inside our journal or hear about what we're sharing?

_____

_____

_____

8. Are there any other guidelines we'd like to establish before we dive in?

_____

_____

_____

SON WRITES
MOM, YOU MAKE ME GRIN WHEN YOU

You being so _____!

And me smiling like a _____!

SON, YOU MAKE ME GRIN WHEN YOU

_____

_____

_____

_____

You being so
_____!

And me smiling like a
_____!

MOM WRITES
THE FOODS I EAT
(and the ones I won't!)

	YUM!	NEVER HAD IT!	IT'S OK.	EWWW GROSS!
Asparagus	☐	☐	☐	☐
Marshmallows	☐	☐	☐	☐
Black licorice	☐	☐	☐	☐
Tomato soup	☐	☐	☐	☐
Brussels sprouts	☐	☐	☐	☐
Cantaloupe	☐	☐	☐	☐
Curry	☐	☐	☐	☐
Candy corn	☐	☐	☐	☐
Olives	☐	☐	☐	☐
Pineapple pizza	☐	☐	☐	☐
Oatmeal	☐	☐	☐	☐
Tofu	☐	☐	☐	☐
Cooked mushrooms	☐	☐	☐	☐
Fruitcake	☐	☐	☐	☐
Pickled pigs' feet	☐	☐	☐	☐
Escargot	☐	☐	☐	☐
Kimchi	☐	☐	☐	☐
Shrimp and grits	☐	☐	☐	☐
Raisin cookies	☐	☐	☐	☐
Gummy worms	☐	☐	☐	☐
Sushi	☐	☐	☐	☐
Trout	☐	☐	☐	☐
Hot sauce	☐	☐	☐	☐

HOT

THE FOODS I EAT

(and the ones I won't!)

DATE

	YUM!	NEVER HAD IT!	IT'S OK.	EWWW GROSS!
Asparagus	☐	☐	☐	☐
Marshmallows	☐	☐	☐	☐
Black licorice	☐	☐	☐	☐
Tomato soup	☐	☐	☐	☐
Brussels sprouts	☐	☐	☐	☐
Cantaloupe	☐	☐	☐	☐
Curry	☐	☐	☐	☐
Candy corn	☐	☐	☐	☐
Olives	☐	☐	☐	☐
Pineapple pizza	☐	☐	☐	☐
Oatmeal	☐	☐	☐	☐
Tofu	☐	☐	☐	☐
Cooked mushrooms	☐	☐	☐	☐
Fruitcake	☐	☐	☐	☐
Pickled pigs' feet	☐	☐	☐	☐
Escargot	☐	☐	☐	☐
Kimchi	☐	☐	☐	☐
Shrimp and grits	☐	☐	☐	☐
Raisin cookies	☐	☐	☐	☐
Gummy worms	☐	☐	☐	☐
Sushi	☐	☐	☐	☐
Trout	☐	☐	☐	☐
Hot sauce	☐	☐	☐	☐

A TYPICAL MONDAY MORNING AT OUR HOUSE

Mom Writes

MOM'S DREAM MONDAY

SON'S DREAM MONDAY

Son Writes

SON WRITES

Music I loved when I was younger

Music I enjoy now

MOM WRITES

Music I loved when I was younger

Music I enjoy now

TOGETHER

We like listening to

DEAR SON,
WHAT WOULD YOU LIKE TO DO THIS SUMMER?

DEAR MOM,

HOW DID YOU SPEND THE SUMMERS WHEN YOU WERE MY AGE?

SON WRITES

HERE'S SOMETHING THIS WEEK THAT

Went well

Challenged me

Brought me stress or anxiety

Cracked me up

Made me feel loved

Frustrated me

MOM WRITES

HERE'S SOMETHING THIS WEEK THAT

Went well

Challenged me

Cracked me up

Brought me stress or anxiety

Made me feel loved

Frustrated me

DEAR SON,

Which school subject is your favorite?

Why do you enjoy it so much?

Why do you think other people struggle with it?

Tell me about something you're working on in this subject.

DEAR MOM,

What are your thoughts on what I wrote about my favorite subject?

Tell me about a subject you loved when you were my age.

SOMETHING I WORKED ON

How does knowing that subject help your life today?

DEAR SON,

I have a question for you:

_____

_____

_____?

SON WRITES

HERE'S A PAGE OF OUR
DIFFERENT DOODLES AND DESIGNS

Mom

Son

Son

Mom

Mom

Son

Son

DEAR MOM,

Tell me a story or two about when I was younger.

SON WRITES

A few things I'll never throw away

MOM WRITES

A few things I'll always keep from your childhood

DEAR SON,

How do you think people your age see you?

How do you think kids younger than you see you?

How do you think adults see you?

How do you think I see you?

Do any of these match how you see yourself?

How does it make you feel when people see you differently than you do?

How do you feel when people see you similarly to how you see yourself?

DEAR MOM,

What are your thoughts on how I believe
other people perceive me?

What do you see when you look at me?

THREE THINGS

I NEVER HAVE THE TIME FOR

SON

1. _____
2. _____
3. _____

MOM

1. _____
2. _____
3. _____

I ALWAYS MAKE TIME FOR

SON

1. _____
2. _____
3. _____

MOM

1. _____
2. _____
3. _____

I ENJOY DOING TOGETHER

SON

1. _____
2. _____
3. _____

MOM

1. _____
2. _____
3. _____

SON WRITES
THIS OR THAT?

Circle each preference

Jeans	Sweats
Big house	Big trip
City	Country
Music	Podcast
Bagel	Donut
Truth	Dare
Shower gel	Soap bar
Comedy	Sci-fi
Roller coaster	Bumper cars
Indiana Jones	Back to the Future
Sour cream	Guacamole
Rich	Famous
Security	Freedom
Book smarts	Street smarts
Football	Baseball
See the future	Change the past

LOL

MOM WRITES
THIS OR THAT?

Jeans	Sweats
Big house	Big trip
City	Country
Music	Podcast
Bagel	Donut
Truth	Dare
Shower gel	Soap bar
Comedy	Sci-fi
Roller coaster	Bumper cars
Indiana Jones	Back to the Future
Sour cream	Guacamole
Rich	Famous
Security	Freedom
Book smarts	Street smarts
Football	Baseball
See the future	Change the past

Include any interesting details!

SON WRITES
PEOPLE I ADMIRE

FRIEND

MENTOR

LOCAL THAT I DON'T KNOW

EDUCATOR

AUTHOR

POLITICIAN

PODCASTER OR VODCASTER

ACTOR

ATHLETE

MUSICIAN

ARTIST

GAMER

MOM WRITES
PEOPLE I ADMIRE

FRIEND

MENTOR

LOCAL THAT I DON'T KNOW

EDUCATOR

AUTHOR

POLITICIAN

PODCASTER OR VODCASTER

ACTOR

ATHLETE

MUSICIAN

ARTIST

GAMER

HERE'S A PICTURE OF
YOU AND ME
WITH OUR ENTIRE FAMILY

YOU KNOW YOU'RE A PART OF OUR FAMILY IF YOU

SAY

EAT

LAUGH ABOUT

ALWAYS NEED TO

TALK ABOUT THE TIME WHEN

APPRECIATE

OUR THEME SONG COULD BE

WE THINK THIS CREW GETS ☆☆☆☆☆ STARS!

DEAR SON,

What do you appreciate about our family?

Is there anything that embarrasses you or that you wish you could change?

How do you know we really love you?

Tell me about a time when you felt proud to be a part of this family.

EPIC

What do you appreciate about our family?

Is there anything that drives you crazy?

Tell me a story about a time when you could see
me being an important part of our family.

THIS IS US

Discovering that we just _____

SON

MOM

Receiving a package from _____

SON

MOM

Cheering for _____

SON

MOM

DEAR SON,

What frightens you about your future?

_____

_____

_____

_____

_____

_____

_____

DEAR MOM,

What do you think about what I wrote?

_____

_____

_____

_____

Did you worry about this when you were my age?

_____

_____

_____

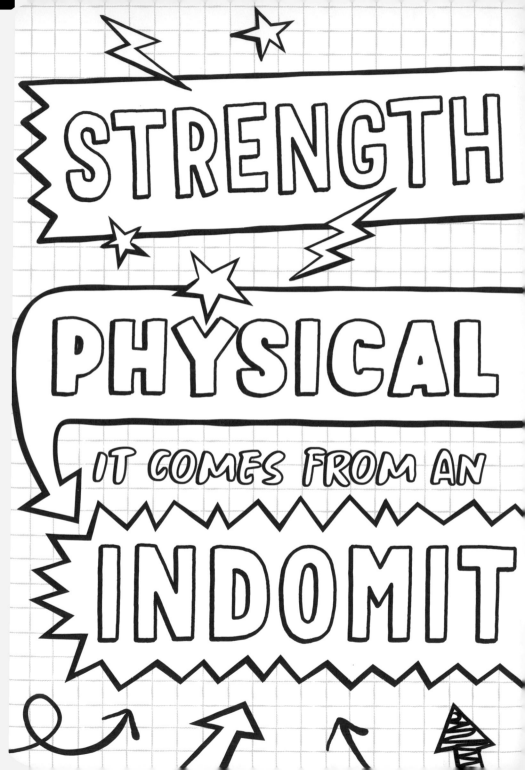

DEAR MOM,

Tell me about a relative that I didn't get to know well.

WE ♥ OUR FAMILY

♥ THIS MEMORY!

DEAR SON,

Tell me about a time when you knew you did the
right thing even though you didn't have to.

Why did you do it?

What did your peers say? Or what do you
imagine they would have said?

Does their opinion matter? Should it?

How did your choice to do the right thing make you feel?

DEAR MOM,

Describe a time when you witnessed me
doing the right thing.

AWESOME!

SON WRITES
MY TYPICAL WEEKDAY

5:00 _____	3:00 _____
6:00 _____	4:00 _____
7:00 _____	5:00 _____
8:00 _____	6:00 _____
9:00 _____	7:00 _____
10:00 _____	8:00 _____
11:00 _____	9:00 _____
NOON _____	10:00 _____
1:00 _____	11:00 _____
2:00 _____	MIDNIGHT _____

My favorite part is

_____
_____
_____
_____
_____

I'm not really a fan of

_____
_____
_____
_____
_____

MOM WRITES
MY TYPICAL WEEKDAY

5:00 _____	3:00 _____
6:00 _____	4:00 _____
7:00 _____	5:00 _____
8:00 _____	6:00 _____
9:00 _____	7:00 _____
10:00 _____	8:00 _____
11:00 _____	9:00 _____
NOON _____	10:00 _____
1:00 _____	11:00 _____
2:00 _____	MIDNIGHT _____

My favorite part is

_____

_____

_____

_____

_____

I'm not really a fan of

_____

_____

_____

_____

_____

SON WRITES

IF I KNEW I COULD NEVER FAIL, I WOULD

1.

2.

3.

4.

5.

MOM WRITES

SON, HERE'S WHAT I KNOW ABOUT FOLLOWING YOUR DREAMS.

_____

_____

_____

_____

_____

_____

_____

_____

_____

_____

_____

_____

_____

_____

_____

_____

I BELIEVE IN YOU

_____

_____

_____

LITTLE THINGS WE'RE GRATEFUL FOR RIGHT NOW

MOM

1.

2.

3.

4.

5.

6.

SON

1.

2.

3.

4.

5.

6.

DEAR MOM,

Do you remember a moment when you felt really loved?
Tell me about it.

Why does this memory matter to you?

DEAR SON,
TELL ME THE STORY OF

_____

_____

EPIC

SON WRITES

If I could bring home any animal in the world, I'd pick a _____ and name it _____.

MOM WRITES

My response would probably be

SON WRITES

And then I'd answer

☐ BTW, we're not getting one!

MOM WRITES

DEAR SON,

What do you think about dating and relationships right now?

Do you have any questions for me?

Do you have anything you want to tell me?

DEAR MOM,

What do you think about what I wrote?

Do you have any words of wisdom?

SON WRITES

The people or groups I message most

1.

2.

3.

The emojis I use most

The last text I sent you, Mom

The last photo or
meme I sent you

MOM WRITES

The people or groups I message most

1.

2.

3.

The emojis I use most

The last text I sent you, Mom

The last photo or meme I sent you

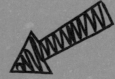

SON WRITES
THIS OR THAT?

Circle each preference

Time	Money
The journey	The destination
Art class	Math class
Pancakes	Waffles
Halloween	New Year's Eve
Wendy's	McDonald's
Meat	Potatoes
The Beatles	The Rolling Stones
Watch sports	Do sports
Corn dog	Cotton candy
Sing	Dance
Superman	Batman
Early	Late
Summer	Winter
East Coast	West Coast
Sweet	Salty

MOM WRITES
THIS OR THAT?

Time	Money
The journey	The destination
Art class	Math class
Pancakes	Waffles
Halloween	New Year's Eve
Wendy's	McDonald's
Meat	Potatoes
The Beatles	The Rolling Stones
Watch sports	Do sports
Corn dog	Cotton candy
Sing	Dance
Superman	Batman
Early	Late
Summer	Winter
East Coast	West Coast
Sweet	Salty

Include any interesting details!

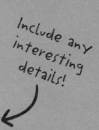

SON WRITES

One day, I'd like to

MY BUCKET LIST

TRY

EAT

CREATE

LEARN

CHANGE

SEE

UNDERSTAND

HELP

CHEER

LOVE

SPEAK WITH

ENJOY

COMPLETE

MOM WRITES

I think that your list is

The item that surprised me is

The one I knew you'd include is

One I'd love to do with you is

SON WRITES

Let me tell you about what I wrote for the word _____

The items that are most important to me (and why) are

1.

2.

DEAR MOM,

Tell me about a decision you made to make my life better,
even though it was difficult for you.

Why did you do it?

How do you feel about that choice today?

DEAR SON,

Tell me about a difficult decision you recently had to make.

How did you ultimately choose what to do?

Why do you think it's important to expose ourselves
to hard situations or opportunities?

CURRENTLY ON MY

BATHROOM SINK

SON

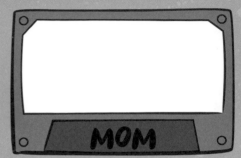

MOM

NIGHTSTAND

SON

MOM

DESK

SON

MOM

DEAR MOM,

WHAT ARE SOME OF YOUR FAVORITE PARTS OF BEING A PARENT RIGHT NOW?

DEAR SON,

Do you ever find yourself being bullied?
Or do you ever pick on any of your peers?

Tell me about a recent experience.

Why do you think it happens?

How does it make you feel about yourself?

DEAR MOM,

What do you think about what I told you?

Do you have any wisdom you could share?

MY PLAYLIST

1.

2.

3.

4.

5.

6.

7.

I enjoy listening to these songs while

Technology I use to listen

MY SIGNATURE DANCE MOVE

TURN THE VOLUME TO

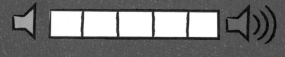

MOM WRITES

I enjoy listening to these songs while

MY PLAYLIST

1.
2.
3.
4.
5.
6.
7.

Technology I use to listen

MY SIGNATURE DANCE MOVE

TURN THE VOLUME TO

DEAR MOM,

What were your parents like when you were my age?

What did you enjoy doing with them?

Was it ever difficult for you to get along?

Tell me about a time when you did something you
weren't supposed to do. How did they respond?

Looking back, how do you know that they loved you so much?

DEAR SON,

What do you think about what I wrote?

Do you think it's easier or more difficult to be a
teenager now versus when I was your age?

DEAR MOM,

Do you think it's easier or more difficult to be a
teenager now versus when you were my age?

How do you think I'm doing?

I GIVE YOU ☆☆☆☆☆ STARS!

DEAR SON,

Tell me a story about a time when you worked really hard at something and succeeded! How did it make you feel?

Tell me a story about a time when you worked really hard and didn't see the results you'd expected.

In hindsight, do you see any benefits to the outcome you experienced?

DEAR MOM,

Do you vote? Why or why not?

What do you think makes a good candidate?

DEAR SON,

What do you think are some great reasons to vote?

What do you think makes a good candidate?

YOUR
VOICE
MATTERS

YOU ★ ME

Things we enjoy doing together

AT HOME

IN OUR COMMUNITY

OUTSIDE

WITH OTHER PEOPLE

COOL

SON WRITES

Mom, you deserve an award for

EXCELLENT

AWESOME!

ROCK ★ STAR

I'm proud to be your son because

WOW

THIS IS US

We lose track of time when

SON

MOM

We are obsessed with

SON

MOM

We always laugh when

SON

MOM

We always forget where

SON

MOM

We get so stubborn about

SON

MOM

We cheer like crazy for

SON

MOM

We always wear

SON

MOM

We're really good at

SON

MOM

We're pretty bad at

SON

MOM

We collect a lot of

SON

MOM

SON WRITES

MOM, HERE'S A T-SHIRT I'M DESIGNING FOR YOU.

MOM WRITES

SON, HERE'S A T-SHIRT I'M DESIGNING FOR YOU.

DEAR SON,

Do you ever feel down, depressed, or hopeless about things in your life? Tell me about it.

Do you ever feel so excited that you think you might burst? Tell me about that.

DEAR MOM,

What's your advice for when life feels hard?

What's your advice for when life feels really good?

SON WRITES

The money we have has enabled our family to

These are times when money doesn't matter to our family

I think it's important to set aside money for

To live within your means is to

I'm currently saving for

Debt becomes a problem when

I enjoy giving time or money to

MOM WRITES

The money we have has enabled our family to

These are times when money doesn't matter to our family

I think it's important to set aside money for

To live within your means is to

I'm currently saving for

Debt becomes a problem when

I enjoy giving time or money to

WE LOVE WHERE WE LIVE BECAUSE

1.

2.

3.

HOME

NEIGHBORHOOD

AROUND HERE, PEOPLE:

Eat_____

Drink_____

Say_____

Wear_____

Never_____

Always_____

Celebrate_____

Do this on weekends_____

Make a big deal about_____

_____

SO DO WE!

	SON	MOM
Eat	☐	☐
Drink	☐	☐
Say	☐	☐
Wear	☐	☐
Never	☐	☐
Always	☐	☐
Celebrate	☐	☐
Do this on weekends	☐	☐
Make a big deal about	☐	☐
	☐	☐

AROUND HERE, WE LIKE GOING TO:

SON

MOM

1.

1.

2.

2.

3.

3.

One area where we think our community could be improved is

One thing we'd never change is

HOME SWEET HOME

DEAR SON,

When you're grown, do you want to stay in our community or live somewhere else? Where would you want to go?

DEAR MOM,

Is there anywhere else you'd like to live one day?

SON WRITES

Mom, I have to admit that you were right about

MOM WRITES

Son, I have to admit that you were right about

DEAR SON,

Do you feel like I'm giving you room to grow?

DEAR MOM,

I have a question for you:

FANTASTIC THINGS WE'VE DONE TOGETHER

1.

2.

3.

4.

5.

6.

7.

8.

9.

10.

11.

12.

13.

WOW

INTERESTING THINGS WE STILL NEED TO DO TOGETHER

EPIC

1.

2.

3.

4.

5.

6.

7.

8.

9.

10.

11.

12.

13.

DEAR SON,

What kind of technology do you use to
communicate with your friends?

Record your current email or username here.

How did you get that name?

What do you like about going online?

What do you dislike?

Do you ever feel pressured or
uncomfortable about anything online?

My go-to device

DEAR MOM,

What kind of technology did you use to communicate with friends when you were my age?

Record your first email address here.

How did you get that address?

Did your parents ever take away your technology privileges when you were my age? Why?

What do you like about going online these days?

What do you dislike?

My go-to device

MOM WRITES

Here's a keepsake from my life right now.

IT'S A

- ☐ ticket stub
- ☐ wrapper
- ☐ quote or poem
- ☐ list or note
- ☐ receipt
- ☐ school paper
- ☐ photo or picture
- ☐ _____

I'm adding it to our journal because

_____

_____

_____

_____

SON WRITES

Here's a keepsake from my life right now.

IT'S A

☐ ticket stub   ☐ receipt

☐ wrapper   ☐ school paper

☐ quote or poem   ☐ photo or picture

☐ list or note   ☐ _____

I'm adding it to our journal because

_____

_____

_____

_____

THE WORLD'S
GREATEST FOODS

MOM   **SON**

1.   1.

2.   2.

3.   3.

WE'RE ALWAYS RUNNING OUT OF

MOM

SON

DURING THE HOLIDAYS, WE'RE OBSESSED WITH EATING

MOM

SON

IN THE SUMMER, WE'LL HAPPILY CONSUME SO MUCH

MOM

SON

SON WRITES

I remember one time when we ☐ ate ☐ made

_____ .

Psst Mom, I'd love to ☐ eat ☐ make

_____ with you again.

MOM WRITES

I remember one time when we ☐ ate ☐ made

_____ .

YUM!

WE WRITE

A Favorite Family Recipe

We call it →

INGREDIENTS	DIRECTIONS
_____	_____
_____	_____
_____	_____
_____	_____
_____	_____
_____	_____
_____	_____
_____	_____
_____	_____

HOT

DEAR SON,

How do you believe girls and women deserve to be treated?

Do you ever see people doing something different?

How do you feel about that?

Do you think there are ways our society should change?

DEAR MOM,

What are your thoughts on what I wrote?

How do you believe girls and women deserve to be treated?

Do you ever see people doing something different?
How do you feel about that?

Has our society changed since you were my age?
Do you think there are ways our society should change now?

DEAR SON,

What's a topic you're afraid to discuss with me?

Why do you think it makes you feel uncomfortable?

Would you like to write it out here?

_____

_____

_____

_____

_____

_____

_____

_____

_____

_____

_____

_____

_____

_____

_____

_____

_____

_____

_____

**Will you come to me when you're ready to talk,
or would you like me to come to you?**

_____

_____

DEAR MOM,

What do you think about everything I just wrote about my emotions?

Do you ever feel nervous to say something out loud?
What do you do?

What's one of the most difficult conversations you've had with someone?

Why was it so hard?

Do you have advice for me when I need to have a hard conversation?

YOU GOT THIS!

THE SUN SHINES NOT ON US BUT IN US

John Muir

DEAR SON,

What do you think this quotation from John Muir means?

On a scale of **1** to **5**,
how much do you feel like you're shining from the inside?

① ② ③ ④ ⑤

What makes you give yourself that rank?

DEAR MOM,

Did you get good grades in school?

How did this influence your life later?

Which subject(s) came easily?

Which subjects were harder or less interesting to you?

DEAR SON,

What do you think about what I wrote?

How are you feeling about your studies?

Is there anything you're struggling with?

Is there something you wish you could do more or less of?

SON WRITES
THIS OR THAT?

Circle each preference

Pen	Pencil
Sweet	Sour
Form	Function
Stay in	Go out
Read the book	Watch the movie
Video chat	Audio chat
Corn chips	Potato chips
Chocolate ice cream	Vanilla ice cream
Morning caffeine	Caffeine-free morning
Board game	Video game
Marvel comics	DC comics
Snow	Sand
Flip flops	Sneakers
Science class	English class
Cake	Pie
Speakers	Headphones or Earbuds

MOM WRITES

THIS OR THAT?

Pen	Pencil
Sweet	Sour
Form	Function
Stay in	Go out
Read the book	Watch the movie
Video chat	Audio chat
Corn chips	Potato chips
Chocolate ice cream	Vanilla ice cream
Morning caffeine	Caffeine-free morning
Board game	Video game
Marvel comics	DC comics
Snow	Sand
Flip flops	Sneakers
Science class	English class
Cake	Pie
Speakers	Headphones or Earbuds

Include any interesting details!

DEAR SON,

Tell me something that makes you feel

Proud

Curious

Relaxed

Angry

Sad

Excited

Anxious

True to Yourself

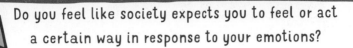

Do you feel like society expects you to feel or act a certain way in response to your emotions?

Why do you think it's like that?

Is there anything I could do to help you with the things you wrote?

DEAR MOM,

What do you think about everything I wrote?

Do you feel like society expects me to feel or act a certain way in response to my emotions? And what do you think about it?

When do you see me being really true to myself?

Tell me about something that makes you feel true to yourself.

YOU GOT THIS!

SON WRITES

Mom, I don't understand why your generation likes to

_____

_____

_____

MOM WRITES

Can you please explain?

MOM WRITES

Son, I don't understand why your generation likes to

_____

_____

_____

Can you please explain?

SON WRITES

DEAR SON,

Hmmm...

If you could add, change, enforce, or eliminate one rule at our house, tell me about what you'd pick.

_____
_____
_____
_____
_____
_____
_____
_____
_____
_____

DEAR MOM,

What do you think?

☐ Sure, let's try it
☐ I hadn't thought of that
☐ Sorry, we can't do that right now
☐ _____

because

_____
_____
_____
_____
_____

MOM WRITES

Son, the world needs to know about your

I love how you

I'm still so impressed that you

One day, I hope you get the chance to

Know I'm always here for you because

DEAR SON,

Tell me the story of

Son Writes

DEAR MOM,

What was probably the most uncharacteristic job you've ever had?

How old were you? And why did you do this job?

What were your responsibilities?

What made the job interesting?

Explain something unexpected that you discovered about yourself.

Tell me about a mistake you made or lesson you learned.

DEAR SON,

What do you think about my job?

Would you try it?

What kind of jobs would you like to explore?

Tell me about the kind of work and life you
dream of having when you're grown.

I BELIEVE
IN YOU

MOM WRITES COOL

I can't get enough of this show

It's fantastic because

The technology I use to watch it is

Here's where I watch it most

I can't get enough of this show

It's fantastic because

The technology I use to watch it is

Here's where I watch it most

MOM WRITES

SON, GIVE YOURSELF PERMISSION TO

say yes to

say no to

put yourself first when

laugh at yourself when

SON WRITES

MOM, GIVE YOURSELF PERMISSION TO

say yes to

say no to

put yourself first when

laugh at yourself when

THIS IS US

Our eat-in-the-car, gotta-be-quick meal

SON

MOM

Our choice restaurant dinner

SON

MOM

Our takes-all-day-to-cook pick for dinner

SON

MOM

Our go-to snack at home

SON

MOM

Our beloved comfort food

SON

MOM